CLAIM the Life

Semester 1

Journey

07 08 09 10 11 12 13 14 15 16—10 9 8 7 6 5 4 3 2 1

Cover Design: Keely Moore

Contents

Journey

> **journey** (JUHR-nee) *n.* The act of traveling from one place to another. *v.* To travel over or through.

"Do you see what this means—all these pioneers who blazed the way, all these veterans cheering us on? It means we'd better get on with it. Strip down, start running—and never quit. No extra spiritual fat, no parasitic sins. Keep your eyes on *Jesus*, who both began and finished this race we're in. Study how he did it. Because he never lost sight of where he was headed—that exhilarating finish in and with God—he could put up with anything along the way: cross, shame, whatever."

Hebrews 12:1-2 (*Message*)

Reflections: Looking Back

What are your thoughts or questions? What images or ideas grabbed your attention? What surprised you?

Connections: Looking Ahead

After talking together about the video, think about these questions. Answer them individually:

1. How does this video relate to your Christian journey?

2. What person did you relate to?

3. Why, do you think, do we need other people on our journey of faith?

4. If you had to make a video of your journey, what people, settings, images, and so forth would you include?

Journey Renewal

In the list below, circle the words that describe your journey with God today.

wandering   roaming   walking   striding

trudging   swaggering   creeping   exploring

sleepwalking   cruising   sneaking   strolling

skipping   running   jogging   galloping

speeding   stalled   at a dead stop

Now, circle the words that describe how you feel about the journey
and where you are in your relationship with God:

confident   assured   hopeful   afraid   nervous

joyful   concerned   wondering   angry

frustrated   happy   doubting   lonely

On the lines below, write a one-sentence prayer asking God to renew you on your journey of faith.

_____

_____

Worship

worship (WUHR-ship) *n.* The reverent love and devotion shown to God. The ceremonies, prayers, or other religious forms by which love for God is shown. *v.* To participate in religious rites of worship.

Yet a time is coming and has now come when the true worshipers will worship the Father in spirit and truth, for they are the kind of worshipers the Father seeks. God is spirit, and [God's] worshipers must worship in spirit and in truth.

John 4:23-24 (NIV)

Reflections

Every Day, Every Way

Everything you do can be an act of worship to our ever-present God. Worship the Lord— every day, every way!

List some daily events where you can experiment with learning to focus on God's presence in your life. Can daily chores or homework be an act of worship? talking to parents? hanging out with friends? running? How do you do those everyday things in your life as worship?

But the time is coming—it has, in fact, come—when what you're called will not matter and where you go to worship will not matter.

It's who you are and the way you live that count before God. Your worship must engage your spirit in the pursuit of truth. That's the kind of people the Father is out looking for: those who are simply and honestly *themselves* before (the Lord) in their worship. God is sheer being itself—Spirit. Those who worship (God) must do it out of their very being, their spirits, their true selves, in adoration.

John 4:23-24 (*Message*)

What I want to remember from today's lesson:

Nehemiah 9:6

You alone are the Lord. You made the heavens, even the highest heavens, and all their starry host, the earth and all that is on it, the seas and all that is in them. You give life to everything, and the multitudes of heaven worship you (NIV).

Psalm 100:2

Worship the Lord with gladness; come into (God's) presence with singing (NRSV).

Romans 12:1

I appeal to you therefore, brothers and sisters, by the mercies of God, to present your bodies as a living sacrifice, holy and acceptable to God, which is your spiritual worship (NRSV).

Colossians 3:17, 23-24

And whatever you do or say, do it as a representative of the Lord Jesus, giving thanks through him to God the Father. . . . Work willingly at whatever you do, as though you were working for the Lord rather than for people. Remember that the Lord will give you an inheritance as your reward, and that the Master you are serving is Christ (NLT).

Revelation 15:4

"Who will not fear you, O Lord, and bring glory to your name? For you alone are holy. All nations will come and worship before you, for your righteous acts have been revealed" (NIV).

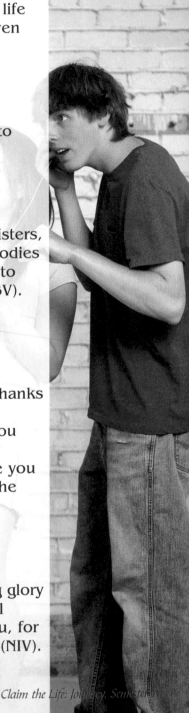

Praying

praying (PRAY-ing) *v.* Speaking to God with words of adoration, confession, thanksgiving, or sincere petition.

ASK.

SEARCH.

KNOCK.

MATTHEW 7:7

Body Prayers

- **Daniel 6:10-11:** "Although Daniel knew that the document had been signed, he continued to go to his house, which had windows in its upper room open toward Jerusalem, and to get down on his knees three times a day to pray to his God and praise him, just as he had done previously. The conspirators came and found Daniel praying and seeking mercy before his God."

- **Nehemiah 8:6:** "Then Ezra blessed the LORD, the great God, and all the people answered, 'Amen, Amen,' lifting up their hands. Then they bowed their heads and worshiped the LORD with their faces to the ground."

- <u>Psalm 141:2</u>: "Let my prayer be counted as incense before you, and the lifting up of my hands as an evening sacrifice."

- <u>Mark 11:25</u>: "Whenever you stand praying, forgive, if you have anything against anyone; so that your Father in heaven may also forgive you your trespasses."

- <u>John 17:1</u>: "After Jesus had spoken these words, he looked up to heaven and said, 'Father, the hour has come; glorify your Son so that the Son may glorify you.'"

God is always speaking to us, but
sometimes our lives are too busy and too noisy
to hear. Praying requires listening as well
as speaking. Spending some time in silence
helps train our ears to hear God's voice.
We can also listen through Scripture,
life circumstances, creation, our bodies,
and other people.

RELATIONSHIP INVENTORY

Answer these questions based on your experience with human relationships:

1. WHAT ARE SOME CHARACTERISTICS OF A HEALTHY RELATIONSHIP?

2. WHAT DOES EACH PERSON HAVE TO DO TO KEEP THE RELATIONSHIP ON GOOD TERMS?

3. WHAT ARE SOME OF THE GIFTS OF BEING PART OF A HEALTHY AND LOVING RELATIONSHIP?

(CONTINUED)

4. WHAT ARE SOME OF THE RISKS AND CHALLENGES OF BEING EMOTIONALLY CLOSE TO SOMEONE?

5. WHEN WE HAVE A DEEP FRIENDSHIP, CAN WE TELL THE OTHER PERSON EXACTLY WHAT WE WANT, WITHOUT LISTENING TO WHAT THE OTHER PERSON WANTS FROM US AND FOR US?

6. WHAT TYPES OF THINGS DO YOU TALK ABOUT WITH YOUR CLOSEST FRIENDS?

7. DO YOU TALK ONLY ABOUT YOURSELF WITH YOUR CLOSE FRIENDS, OR DO YOU ALSO SHARE YOUR CONCERNS AND HOPES FOR OTHER PEOPLE?

8. ARE YOU THE KIND OF FRIEND WHO DOES ALL THE TALKING AND NEVER LETS YOUR FRIEND GET A WORD IN EDGEWISE?

9. DO YOU TAKE TIME TO TELL YOUR CLOSE FRIENDS HOW MUCH THEY MEAN TO YOU AND HOW GRATEFUL YOU ARE FOR THEIR CARE AND SUPPORT?

10. ARE YOU THE KIND OF FRIEND WHO CALLS PEOPLE ONLY WHEN YOU NEED THEM?

11. ARE YOU THE KIND OF FRIEND WHO IS ALWAYS TRYING TO PLEASE YOUR FRIENDS AND NEVER GIVING THEM A CHANCE TO KNOW YOU OR TELL YOU HOW MUCH THEY CARE FOR YOU?

12. DO YOU FIND IT EASY OR HARD TO ASK YOUR FRIENDS FOR HELP, OR TO ADMIT WHEN YOU'VE MADE A MISTAKE, OR TO SHARE THE THINGS THAT MAKE YOU HAPPY?

Now, look over these questions again and imagine that the friendship is between you and God. What things do you discover about how you relate to God?

Put a cross beside those areas where you would like to do more to grow closer to God. How do your answers either affirm or suggest different prayer methods for you to practice?

Image of God

image (IM-ij) *n.* Form; appearance; semblance; likeness.

Then God said, "Let us make humankind in our image, according to our likeness."

(Genesis 1:26a)

Vincent Van Gogh

1. After studying Vincent Van Gogh's artwork on this page and the next, how would you describe the artist?

2. How is his personality reflected in his artwork?

Praising God,
CURSING OTHERS

"NO ONE CAN TAME THE TONGUE—
A RESTLESS EVIL, FULL OF DEADLY
POISON. WITH IT WE BLESS THE LORD
AND FATHER, AND WITH IT WE CURSE
THOSE WHO ARE MADE IN THE
LIKENESS OF GOD" (JAMES 3:8-9).

1. In what ways do we "curse" other people? Think of both words and actions. What are some examples?

2. Why do we praise God but "curse" other people?

3. When we "curse" others, we are denying that they are made in the image of God. When we "curse" others, how do we affect God's image in us?

4. Think about what you've learned about God's image. Why would James specifically point to the tongue as "full of deadly poison"?

5. We bear God's image. How should knowing that cause us to treat ourselves and others differently?

Commitment

commitment (kuh-MIT-ment) *n.* An agreement or pledge to do something.

 "Courage is not being unafraid. Courage is remaining committed to your beliefs even when you are terrified."

"The true test of our faith in God comes when we are challenged to abandon it."

What Would You Do?

Many years ago, a Babylonian king built a ninety-foot statue and ordered all the people of the land to bow down and worship it. Almost everyone did. Three men, however, refused to worship the statue. The king threatened to throw them to their death in a fiery furnace if they did not obey him. If you were one of these three men, what would you do?

A soldier in a battle zone has been captured. His captors threaten him, saying they will behead him if he does not renounce his beliefs and publicly profess faith in their religion. If you were this soldier, what would you do?

Your youth leader has planned an important kick-off event for your group. Guest leaders have been invited, and lots of food has been purchased. You said you would go but, at the last minute, you have been invited to a game to watch your favorite team play ball. What will you do?

You made plans to attend a Christian rock concert Saturday night. Your friends show no interest in Christianity, and you have even heard them make fun of people who go to church. One of your friends asks what you are going to do this weekend. You don't want your friends to think that you aren't like them, but you also have your beliefs. What will you do?

Create your own scenario:

Three Men and a Fiery Furnace
(Daniel 3)

King and Advisors

1. Why do you think the king ordered a ninety-foot statue built?

2. Why do you think the king ordered everyone to worship his statue?

3. How do you think the king felt at the beginning of the story? in the middle? at the end?

4. Have you ever tried to force someone to do things your way? What happened?

Shadrach, Meshach, Abednego

1. Why do you think these men refused to worship the statue?

2. Could they have done something else that would have kept them out of trouble? If so, what are some possibilities?

3. What happened in the end?

4. Have you ever had to stand up for your beliefs? If so, what happened?

People of Babylon

1. Why do you think most people obeyed the king's orders?

2. Do you think they truly believed that worshipping the statue would make a difference? Why, or why not?

3. How do you think they felt at the end of the story?

4. When have you done something just because someone pressured you to do it?

Follow

> **follow** (FAH-loh) *v.* 1. To go, proceed, or come after. 2. To be guided by. 3. To accept the guidance, command, or leadership of. 4. To take as a model; imitate.

Then [Jesus] told [the disciples] what they could expect for themselves: "Anyone who intends to come with me has to let me lead. You're not in the driver's seat—I am. Don't run from suffering; embrace it. Follow me and I'll show you how. Self-help is no help at all. Self-sacrifice is the way, *my* way, to finding yourself, your true self. What good would it do to get everything you want and lose you, the real you?"

—Luke 9:23-25 (Message)

I Will Follow Jesus

- Where in my life do I need to remember to follow Jesus—not to follow other people or my personal desires?

What Did He Mean?

Verse 24: "For those who want to save their life will lose it, and those who lose their life for my sake will save it."

Often Jesus spoke in ways that had more than one meaning. For example, in this one verse, we can understand Jesus' scenario literally. What would that mean? Here's a hint: Think about where the early Christians were persecuted; now, think about Christians who are persecuted today, especially in other countries.

• Write in your own words what you think Jesus is saying if we understand it literally:

• How would that statement be helpful to Christians who are persecuted?

We can also take Jesus' statement as a metaphor, standing for another level of meaning. What might he mean that would apply to us in our daily lives? Here's a hint: Think about who the leader is in each part of the paradox.

• Put into your own words what you think Jesus is saying about the rewards of following each of the two different leaders.

Verse 25: "What does it profit them if they gain the whole world, but lose or forfeit themselves?"

• What kinds of things would you want if someone were to say to you, "You can have the whole world"? List some of the things that you would like to possess:

(Continued)

• From what you know about life, are people who have everything they want automatically happy?

• Where do people find true fulfillment and joy in life?

Verse 23: "If any want to become my followers, let them deny themselves and take up their cross daily and follow me."

• What do you think Jesus means by this statement?

• If you are choosing to follow Jesus, how often do you need to make that decision? Why?

Temple

Temple (TEM-puhl) *n.* A building for religious practice; if capitalized, either of two successive national sanctuaries in ancient Jerusalem used as the primary center for Jewish worship.

DO YOU NOT KNOW . . .

that your body is a temple of the Holy Spirit within you, which you have from God, and that you are not your own? For you were bought with a price; therefore glorify God in your body.

1 Corinthians 6:19-20

☞ Given what you know about the Temple, what do you think Paul means by saying "your body is a temple of the Holy Spirit"?

☞ Paul says "you are not your own. You have been bought with a price." What was the price that was paid?

☞ According to God's Word, how much are you worth?

☞ What does that say about how you should see yourself and treat your body?

Claim the Life: Journey, Semester 1

MIXED UP

WHAT HAPPENED? HOW
DID YOU FEEL AS YOU WATCHED?
WHAT DO YOU THINK?

Taking Care of My Temple

God values you so much that your body is a dwelling place of God's Holy Spirit.

Write five things you will do to take care of your body.

Write five things that you will avoid because they are harmful to your body.

Forgiving

> **forgiving** (for-GIV-ing) *adj.* Willing or able to give up resentment of or claim to retaliation for.

One day he was praying in a certain place. When he finished, one of his disciples said, "Master, teach us to pray just as John taught his disciples."

So he said, "When you pray, say,

Father,

Reveal who you are.

Set the world right.

Keep us alive
   with three square meals.

**Keep us forgiven with you
   and forgiving others.**

Keep us safe from ourselves
   and the Devil."

—Luke 11:1-4 (*Message*)

And Now, A Word From Our Sponsor

The Announcer begins (*in the upbeat tone of a TV commercial*):

Are you carrying around grudges against others? (**Helper 1** *acts out carrying something heavy on his or her back. When the next question begins, he or she freezes in place.*)

Do you ever find yourself irritable or angry when you think about those people? (**Helper 2** *looks annoyed and then freezes in place.*)

Do you feel hurt or sad about the loss of a friendship, or put-down by what someone else said about you? (**Helper 1** *gets down on one knee, rests an elbow on the other knee, and hides his or her face in both hands.*)

Well . . . have we got an answer for you! (**The helpers** *jump up, look at announcer, and look astonished.*)

It's called FORGIVING. (**Helper 2** *holds up a sign that says FORGIVING.*)

Extensive testing has been done on this; and many who use it have found that it relieves nagging heartaches, soothes your weary soul, and lightens your footsteps by releasing the negative vibes that keep you grumpy.

So, don't wait another day! The sooner you start, the better you'll feel! (**Helper 1** *jumps up and down for joy then freezes.*)

Call God today! God is standing by and ready to take your phone call, ready to deliver forgiveness directly to you so that you can begin using it yourself—and reap great benefits! (**Helper 2** *holds hands together in prayer and looks up.*)

So, start right now and see for yourself how amazing forgiving can be! (**The helpers** *shake hands with each other and then walk off together.*)

IN MY LIFE

▶ IS THERE SOMEONE IN YOUR LIFE, OR PREVIOUSLY IN YOUR LIFE, WHOM YOU NEED TO FORGIVE?

▶ IS THERE SOMEONE YOU WISH WOULD FORGIVE YOU? HAVE YOU ASKED FOR FORGIVENESS?

▶ WRITE YOUR THOUGHTS ABOUT THIS QUOTATION:

"IT IS EASIER TO FORGIVE AN ENEMY
THAN TO FORGIVE A FRIEND."
—WILLIAM BLAKE

WHAT COULD YOU DO ?

. WHAT COULD YOU DO TO SHOW LOVE (RESPECT) TO SOMEONE EVEN IF YOU HAVE HAD A NEGATIVE EXPERIENCE WITH HIM OR HER IN THE PAST?

. WHAT COULD YOU DO TO HELP YOU FORGIVE SOMEONE WHEN YOU CAN'T FORGET WHAT HAPPENED?

MAY GOD, WHO FORGIVES US, CHANGES US, AND LOVES US NO MATTER WHAT, HELP US TO FORGIVE AND LOVE OTHERS AS GOD LOVES US.

Kindness

> **kindness** (KIGHND-nis) *n.* The state or quality of being friendly, generous, or warmhearted.

KINDNESS CAN BECOME ITS OWN MOTIVE. WE ARE
MADE KIND BY BEING KIND.

\- ERIC HOFFER

KIND WORDS CAN BE SHORT AND EASY TO SPEAK,
BUT THEIR ECHOES ARE TRULY ENDLESS.

\- MOTHER TERESA

CONSTANT KINDNESS CAN ACCOMPLISH MUCH. AS
THE SUN MAKES ICE MELT, KINDNESS CAUSES
MISUNDERSTANDING, MISTRUST, AND HOSTILITY
TO EVAPORATE.

\- ALBERT SCHWEITZER

KIND WORDS DO NOT COST MUCH. YET THEY
ACCOMPLISH MUCH.

\- BLAISE PASCAL

REMEMBER THERE'S NO SUCH THING AS A SMALL ACT
OF KINDNESS. EVERY ACT CREATES A RIPPLE WITH
NO LOGICAL END.

\- SCOTT ADAMS

THE LITTLE UNREMEMBERED ACTS OF KINDNESS AND LOVE ARE THE BEST PARTS OF A PERSON'S LIFE.

- WILLIAM WORDSWORTH

THREE THINGS IN HUMAN LIFE ARE IMPORTANT. THE FIRST IS TO BE KIND. THE SECOND IS TO BE KIND. THE THIRD IS TO BE KIND.

- HENRY JAMES

KINDNESS IN WORDS CREATES CONFIDENCE.

KINDNESS IN THINKING CREATES PROFUNDITY.

KINDNESS IN GIVING CREATES LOVE.

- LAO-TSE

WHEN YOU CARRY OUT ACTS OF KINDNESS YOU GET A WONDERFUL FEELING INSIDE. IT IS AS THOUGH SOMETHING INSIDE YOUR BODY RESPONDS AND SAYS, YES, THIS IS HOW I OUGHT TO FEEL.

- HAROLD KUSHNER

Our Offering to God

✍ List examples of behaviors in these categories:

Showing Kindness – versus – That Stinks!

✍ Whom do you find it hard to be kind to?

✍ When is it hard to be kind?

✍ What acts of kindness can you do to take a something that "stinks" and turn it into a pleasing offering to God?

SOMETIMES YOU MAY FIND YOURSELF IN A SITUATION OR CONVERSATION THAT ISN'T GOING WELL OR HAS THE POTENTIAL OF TURNING NASTY.
IN THE FOLLOWING SCENARIOS, IDENTIFY LIKELY CONSEQUENCES OF BEING NASTY VERSUS BEING KIND.

- SOMEONE CUTS IN FRONT OF YOU IN THE LINE TO BUY MOVIE TICKETS.

- SOMEONE TRIES TO PICK A FIGHT WITH YOU AT THE BUS STOP.

- AS YOU PASS A GROUP OF KIDS IN THE MALL, THEY LAUGH AT YOU.

- YOU SEE SOMEONE TEASING A FRIEND OF YOURS AT SCHOOL.

- A TEACHER QUESTIONS IF YOU LOOKED AT SOMEONE ELSE'S PAPER DURING A TEST.

- YOUR PARENTS ASK YOU WHERE YOU ARE GOING AND WHAT TIME YOU WILL BE BACK.

Practice Makes Perfect (Almost)

We can intentionally change our behavior, but it takes practice. Here are some things you can try to help you be more aware and choose to be kind, even when you don't feel like being kind. What other ideas can you add to the list?

- Count to 5 before answering someone by making a rude remark.

- Make the effort to ask a question that will begin a brief conversation with someone you don't really want to talk to.

- Take time to listen to someone.

- Look for ways you can help another person—carry a heavy bag, open a door, send a card to someone who is ill.

   - Smile at people you pass when walking down a school hallway or at the mall.

      - Give genuine compliments to others.

      - Be polite to your server at a restaurant.

      - Greet the clerk in a checkout line.

      - Turn off your cell phone or turn it to silent while you are in class or a meeting.

HALT for Kindness

Being kind to yourself and others is a choice. One way to remind yourself to make the right choice is to develop an acronym or phrase that will help you at the point of decision. Try using the word HALT.

When persons are . . .

Hungry
Angry
Lonely
Tired

. . . they are less likely to treat others with kindness.

You may find yourself in one of those conditions, or you may realize that the person with whom you are dealing is acting out of hunger or tiredness, for example. Those factors are not an excuse to treat others with less than kindness. But if you HALT, you can stop and think about how you will respond. Just think the word HALT, and ask God for direction.

What one thing can you do this week to be more kind to others?

_____

_____

Servant

servant (SUHR-vuhnt) *n.* 1. One who expresses submission or debt to another. 2. One who performs duties about the person or home of a master or personal employer.

Did You Know . . . ?

The word *servant* actually means several different things. Did you know that it stands for . . .

◉ A person hired to do jobs for another person (usually household work)

◉ A Christian rock band from the 1970s

◉ An alternative rock band based in London, England

◉ A 1963 British film about a young bachelor and the man who worked for him

◉ The name of an airline operating in southwestern Alaska

◉ The name of a ministry that purports to "go where God says to go and do what God says to do"

◉ The name of a center that serves disabled homeless men

◉ The name of the publication of poetry, meditations, and news from a religious community called The Brotherhood of Saint Gregory

What Did Jesus Do? ⓐ

Across

3. Who was gathered around the table with Jesus?
5. No servant is greater than his _____.
6. This dinner was important because it would turn out to be their last one _____.
8. It was just before what feast?
9. Jesus said that if you do these things, you will be

   _____.

Down

1. Who was the disciple urged to betray Jesus?
2. Who was encouraging that disciple (number 1 Down) to betray Jesus?
4. Which disciple did not want Jesus to wash his feet?
6. What is one of the names the disciples called Jesus?
7. Jesus said that he washed his feet as an _____ for them.
10. Jesus showed us that each of us should be a _____.
11. This story took place on the night before Jesus _____.

Servant Leaders

Some companies like Starbucks and Southwest Airlines practice a leadership style called "servant leadership." Employees start out as servants and then can become leaders in the business. Basic principles of servant-leadership rely on listening (to what others say as well as to what they don't say), empathizing (recognizing others' value and accepting who they are as people), persuading (working toward an understanding with others without using undue power or authoritarian techniques), and building community (working toward a positive working relationship among all employees, developing that into a true team spirit). By the way, lots of churches and youth groups practice this style of leadership too!

How well would you do working for one of these organizations? Take this quiz:

Listening

____a. No way!

____b. Once in a while

____c. I **CAN** when I want to

____d. Pretty good most of the time

____e. People say I am really good at this!

Empathizing

____a. I wish people would just accept my point of view.

____b. Most of the time I'm not very accepting of others.

____c. Most of the time I understand where people are coming from, but there are a few people that really get me going.

____d. I'm pretty good at understanding other people's points of view.

____e. I consider myself very tolerant and accepting of other people.

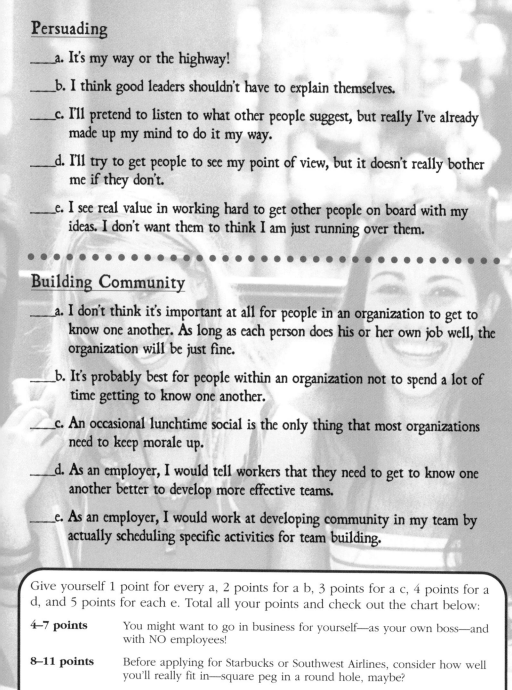

Persuading

____a. It's my way or the highway!

____b. I think good leaders shouldn't have to explain themselves.

____c. I'll pretend to listen to what other people suggest, but really I've already made up my mind to do it my way.

____d. I'll try to get people to see my point of view, but it doesn't really bother me if they don't.

____e. I see real value in working hard to get other people on board with my ideas. I don't want them to think I am just running over them.

Building Community

____a. I don't think it's important at all for people in an organization to get to know one another. As long as each person does his or her own job well, the organization will be just fine.

____b. It's probably best for people within an organization not to spend a lot of time getting to know one another.

____c. An occasional lunchtime social is the only thing that most organizations need to keep morale up.

____d. As an employer, I would tell workers that they need to get to know one another better to develop more effective teams.

____e. As an employer, I would work at developing community in my team by actually scheduling specific activities for team building.

Give yourself 1 point for every a, 2 points for a b, 3 points for a c, 4 points for a d, and 5 points for each e. Total all your points and check out the chart below:

4–7 points   You might want to go in business for yourself—as your own boss—and with NO employees!

8–11 points   Before applying for Starbucks or Southwest Airlines, consider how well you'll really fit in—square peg in a round hole, maybe?

12–15 points   Check out the Internet for some articles about servant-leadership. You probably would be a good candidate but need a few pointers.

16–20 points   The Harvard Business School is probably looking for you to help teach and develop courses on servant-leadership! Submit your application. Your Sunday school teacher will give you a great recommendation!

Suffering

suffering (SUHF-er-ing, SUHF-ring) *n*. The condition of one who bears pain or distress.

The Western Wall in Jerusalem is believed to be the largest remaining portion of the Second Temple, which stood at the time of Jesus. It is at the site of the original Temple built by King Solomon. Also known as the Wailing Wall, this ancient remnant is considered to be one of the holiest places on earth. Over the years, the Wailing Wall has become an important place for Jews and others to visit and pray. Traditionally, pilgrims bring their prayer requests written on scraps of paper and squeeze them into cracks in the wall as they pray. This photograph in the background shows the prayer messages in between the ancient stones.

THE CURE

Draw lines between the
sufferings and the cures people
use in each situation.

SUFFERINGS

MOVING

SICKNESS

NO MONEY

PERSONAL PROBLEMS

RELATIONSHIP ISSUES

HURT

LACK OF
    UNDERSTANDING

LONELINESS

INJUSTICE

WAR

CURES

EDUCATION

FORGET ABOUT IT

COUNSELING

PEACE

SUE

MAKE FRIENDS

MEDS

WELFARE

WAR

DRUGS

ALCOHOL

GET INVOLVED

PRAYER

WHAT WE BELIEVE
ABOUT SUFFERING

- GOD DOES NOT CAUSE SUFFERING. WHAT KINDS OF THINGS DO CAUSE SUFFERING?

- GOD IS WITH US, HELPING US THROUGH OUR TIMES OF SUFFERING. HOW HAVE YOU OR OTHERS YOU KNOW EXPERIENCED GOD'S PRESENCE AND HELP IN THE MIDST OF SUFFERING?

- GOD IS AT WORK TO BRING GOOD OUT OF BAD; GOD IS ALWAYS WORKING TOWARD WHOLENESS AND HEALING. WHEN YOU LOOK BACK ON A HARD TIME, WHAT EVIDENCE CAN YOU SEE OF SOMETHING GOOD COMING OUT OF THE EXPERIENCE?

- GOD USES US AS PART OF THE SOLUTION. WE CAN HELP OTHERS WHO SUFFER. WHEN YOU OR SOMEONE YOU KNOW HAS SUFFERED, HOW DID OTHER PEOPLE HELP YOU? HOW HAVE YOU HELPED SOMEONE?

BIBLICAL CURES

LOOK UP YOUR PASSAGE AND NOTE YOUR ANSWERS:

PSALM 32:3-7   MATTHEW 26:36-41

ACTS 7:54-60   2 CORINTHIANS 12:7B-10

• WHAT WAS THE SUFFERING THAT WAS GOING ON?

• WHAT DOES SCRIPTURE SUGGEST AS THE CURE FOR THE SUFFERING?

• WHAT CLUES ARE IN THE PASSAGE FOR US TO USE WHEN WE SUFFER?

Suffering

Endurance

> **endurance** (en-DOOR-uhns, en-DYOOR-uhns) *n.* The act, quality, ability, or power to withstand hardship, stress, or adversity.

"Patient endurance attaineth to all things; who God possesseth in nothing is wanting; alone God sufficeth."

—St Teresa of Avila

Even though I walk
    through the darkest valley,
  I fear no evil;
for you are with me;
  your rod and your staff—
  they comfort me.

—Psalm 23:4

The alternative to enduring is to give up.

God doesn't remove the hard times from the lives of people just because they are Christian disciples, but we are reminded over and over again that God is always with us through those hard times. We can endure.

ENDURANCE:
MY QUOTATION

"Jesus Pulled Me Out"

What kinds of suffering did the interviewees talk about? Make a list.

Choose one person on the video (for example, the man who was a refugee, the man who had lost his legs, the young woman who went through depression, the woman who had bipolar disease.

- IMAGINE HIS OR HER LIFE AND SUFFERING. WHAT DO YOU THINK THAT HAS BEEN LIKE?

- WHAT SEEMS TO HAVE HELPED?

- WHAT ROLE DOES FAITH PLAY IN ENDURING?

ENDURANCE

Be patient, therefore, beloved, until the coming of the Lord. The farmer waits for the precious crop from the earth, being patient with it until it receives the early and the late rains. You also must be patient. Strengthen your hearts, for the coming of the Lord is near. Beloved, do not grumble against one another so that you may not be judged. See the Judge is standing at the doors! As an example of suffering and patience, beloved, take the prophets who spoke the name of the Lord. Indeed we call blessed those who showed endurance. You have heard of the endurance of Job, and you have seen the purpose of the Lord, how the Lord is compassionate and merciful.

(James 5:7-11)

Purity

purity (PYOOR-i-te) *n.* 1. The condition or quality of being pure, not mixed; freedom from anything that contaminates, adulterates, or defiles. 2. moral uprightness, which excludes all impurity of spirit, manner, or act.

Prayer of Purity

Dear God,

Deliver me from
attachment to things unclean
from wrong associations
from the predominance of evil passions
from the sugar of sin as well as its gap
that with . . . deep contrition, and earnest heart searching

I may come to you,
cast myself on you,
   trust in you,
   cry to you,
   be delivered by you.

Because of Christ's purity and in him I pray,
Amen.

Adapted from "Purification" from *The Valley of Vision*, by Arthur Bennett

Scientific Observations: Oil & Water

What are real-life temptations and actions that are inconsistent with being a follower of Christ? Give names to the "colors" red, yellow, green, and blue that try to make your life "muddy and black."

- Red
- Green

- Yellow
- Blue

How do you relate to the first experiment? Where in your life or in the lives of others have you seen the effects of impure living?

In the second experiment, how would you relate the olive oil to your Christian experience? What does the olive oil represent for you? How is the olive oil like knowing you are a beloved child of God?

What actions or attitudes do you believe make your life less than pure?

What in your life, like the olive oil, helps you resist the various things that try to taint your soul?

How can you strengthen those things that help you live in purity?

DEFINE THE WORDS

What is purity?

Team #1: defilement

Team #2: contaminate

Team #3: adulterate

Team #4: moral uprightness

SCRIPTURE SEARCH

Read the following Scriptures and answer the questions below each. In your Bibles, read the verses before and after the printed verses for additional information. Discuss your answers with team members, then be prepared to discuss the questions and answers in the large group.

1. "And all who have this hope in him purify themselves, just as he is pure" (1 John 3:3).

a. To what is "this hope" referring?

b. Who is "him"?

c. What does it mean to purify yourself?

d. Why should you seek purity in life?

2. "Since we have these promises, beloved, let us cleanse ourselves from every defilement of body and of spirit, making holiness perfect in the fear of God" (2 Corinthians 7:1).

a. What are "these promises"?

b. Who are the "beloved"?

(continued))

c. What is an example of defilement of body?

d. What is an example of defilement of spirit?

e. What is the "fear of God"?

f. How do you cleanse yourself from defilement?

g. Why does cleansing yourself from defilement lead to holiness?

3. "Blessed are the pure in heart, for they will see God" (Matthew 5:8).

a. How do the pure in heart see God?

b. What kinds of attitudes and actions come from an impure heart?

courage (KUHR-ij) *n.* The mental or moral strength or quality to venture, persevere, and face danger, fear, or difficulty; bravery.

Wait for the LORD;
   be strong, and let your heart
      take courage;
Wait for the LORD!

               —Psalm 27:14

One isn't necessarily born with courage, but one is born with potential. Without courage, we cannot practice any other virtue with consistency. We can't be kind, true, merciful, generous, or honest.—Maya Angelou

Courage without conscience is a wild beast.—Robert G. Ingersoll

Courage is fear that has said its prayers.—Dorothy Bernard

Courage is being scared to death—but saddling up anyway.—John Wayn

It is curious that physical courage should be so common in the world and moral courage so none. —Mark Twain

Be courageous. Be independent. Only remember where the true courage and independence come from.
—Phillips Brooks

One man with courage makes a majority.
—Andrew Jackson

There is, in addition to a courage with which men die, a courage by which men must live.
—John F. Kennedy

It often requires more courage to dare to do right than to fear to do wrong.
—Abraham Lincoln

It takes as much courage to have tried and failed as it does to have tried and succeeded.
—Anne Morrow Lindbergh

True courage is not the brutal force of vulgar heroes, but the firm resolve of virtue and reason.
—Alfred North Whitehead

64

Giants

We all face "giants" in our lives—things we fear or that threaten us in some way. Your giant may be a bully at school or a life-threatening illness or fear that someone won't like you if you don't do some certain thing. Other "giants" we face are temptations from our culture to worship something other than the one, true God. (This was true for the Israelites when they began living in the Promised Land.) Whatever appeals to you so much that it's crowding out God as the center of your life is another "giant."

Whatever your giants are, it takes courage such as Joshua's in order to face them. In the space provided, name your giants. Then write what you think it means to follow God's way and be courageous in facing those giants.

Giants I face are ...

I will have courage and do ...

Simplicity

> **simplicity** (sim-PLIS-i-tee) *n.* The property, condition, or quality of being of humble origin or modest position; clarity of expression.

"AND CAN ANY OF YOU
BY WORRYING ADD
A SINGLE HOUR
TO YOUR SPAN OF LIFE?"
(MATTHEW 6:27)

"ARE NOT FIVE SPARROWS SOLD FOR TWO PENNIES?
YET NOT ONE OF THEM IS FORGOTTEN BY GOD.
INDEED, THE VERY HAIRS OF YOUR HEAD ARE ALL NUMBERED.
DON'T BE AFRAID; YOU ARE WORTH MORE THAN MANY SPARROWS."
(LUKE 12:6-7)

"KEEP YOUR LIVES FREE FROM THE LOVE OF MONEY,
AND BE CONTENT WITH WHAT YOU HAVE;
FOR HE HAS SAID,
'I WILL NEVER LEAVE YOU OR FORSAKE YOU'"
(HEBREWS 13:5)

? What's it like to be without your "stuff"?

"I WAS LEARNING . . .
THAT A MAN CAN LIVE PROFOUNDLY
WITHOUT MASSES OF THINGS."

–RICHARD E. BYRD
ARCTIC EXPLORER
THE CLASSIC POLAR ADVENTURE

A CHALLENGE

"SIMPLIFY, SIMPLIFY, SIMPLIFY."

—THOREAU

IS THERE SOMETHING YOU OWN THAT YOU FEEL YOU JUST CAN'T GET RID OF?

WHAT IF YOU HAD TO DO WITHOUT IT?

EXPERIMENT WITH THIS IDEA: GO ONE DAY WITHOUT A COMPUTER, PHONE, TV, OR SOME OTHER ITEM OR ACTIVITY YOU DEPEND ON. WHAT DO YOU THINK THIS EXPERIENCE WILL BE LIKE FOR YOU?

ARE THERE OTHER ITEMS THAT YOU COULD GIVE UP? FOR ONE DAY? FOR GOOD?

Count Them Up

My Stuff	How Many?	My Stuff	How Many?
backpacks	3	cell phones/iPods	3
pencils/pens	30	sports equipment	4
notebooks	10	shoes/sports shoes	2
sleepwear	5	pants/shorts/skirts	4
boxes of cereal	4	shirts/sweaters	20
cans of soda	10	uniforms	1
computers	2	coats	3
electronic games	15	books	100
gaming devices	3	board games	4
TVs	1	pieces of jewelry	1
CDs	50	pillows/blankets	15
CD players	0	chairs	3
DVDs	10	cars	1
DVD players	1	bikes/scooters	1
mp3 downloads	sec	collections	2

Goodness

> **Goodness** (GOOD-nis) *n.* The quality or state of being morally excellent, virtuous, righteous, kind, generous, or friendly.

"I desire that . . . those who have come to believe in God may be careful to devote themselves to good works; these things are excellent and profitable to everyone."

——Titus 3:8

UNDERSTANDING GOOD WORKS

1. What is a good work?

2. What are some examples of good works?

3. Why do you call the things you listed in #2 a "good work"?

4. Why does God's Word instruct believers to devote themselves to good works?

5. What happens when followers of Christ are mean, rude, or ignore the needs of others? What do others think when some Christians choose not to do good works?

Good Works for the Living Water

So, how does the water-pass relay at the beginning of class time relate to devoting yourself to good works?

Since Jesus is called the Living Water, think about the water in the full bucket as representing Jesus and all that he has done, all that he has commanded, and all that he means to you.

Think of the smaller cups of water being passed to others from members of the body of Christ. When we are devoted to the call of Christ, the task is easier. We are not perfect, so sometimes a little water spills.

These cupfuls of water being passed down the line represent good works of all kinds. A good work is anything that demonstrates the love of Christ and that brings glory to God.

The full bucket at the end of the line can represent the gospel reaching all corners of the earth. God gives us the tools we need to do these good works. Working together, devoted to proclaiming Christ in the form of good works, accomplishes what God calls us to do!

Pass It On

What are ways you can pass on your "Cup of Good Works" to a person who needs it?

In the space below, make a list of needs you can think of, how you can respond with the love of Christ, and the tools of the Christian faith that can help you meet the needs.

Need	My Response	Tools I Need

What will it take for you to become devoted to good works? What do you need to pass on the Living Water? Write a prayer asking God to make you devoted to good works.

74

DEVOTED TO GOOD WORKS

Write an acrostic poem.

Each line of an acrostic poem must begin with one letter of the topic word and must describe the topic word. Below is an example of an acrostic poem:

D-darling pet

O-obedient, most of the time

G-good friend

What are you devoted to? Consider what you are passionate about, you strongly like, or you hold beliefs about. Write your acrostic poem.

D

E

V

O

T

E

D

WORDS ABOUT THE WORD

Read the following verses about doing good works. Highlight any words that jump out as being significant in explaining devotion to good works for you. When you've read each verse, go back through the highlighted words and make notes below about anything new you've learned.

- "'Let your light shine before others, so that they may see your good works and give glory to your Father in heaven'" (Matthew 5:16).

- "[May you be] filled with the knowledge of God's will in all spiritual wisdom and understanding, so that you may lead lives worthy of the Lord, fully pleasing to [the Lord], as you bear fruit in every good work and as you grow in the knowledge of God" (Colossians 1:9-10).

- "And let us consider how to provoke one another to love and good deeds" (Hebrews 10:24).

- "Now in Joppa there was a disciple whose name was Tabitha, which in Greek is Dorcas. She was devoted to good works and acts of charity" (Acts 9:36).

WHAT HAVE YOU LEARNED ABOUT BEING DEVOTED TO GOOD WORKS FROM THE BIBLE VERSES ABOVE?

Dear God…

Write a letter to God, confessing your neglect of needs around you and of having devotion to things other than good works. Ask God to help you see the needs and to desire to do good works that bring glory to God.

CELEBRATE YOUR JOURNEY

Across

3. Step out in faith and keep going.
4. Take up your cross and _____ me.
5. We _____ in spirit and truth.
6. Freedom from anything that contaminates or defiles
7. Everyone experiences _____, but God is still at work.
9. _____ is speaking and listening to God.
10. Daniel's friends showed great _____ to God.
13. Jesus did the icky job to show us how to live as a _____.
15. Our family resemblance
16. Acts of _____ often turn around something that "stinks"!

Down

1. Your body is the _____ of the Lord.
2. Like Joshua, we are called to act with _____.
8. How many times are we to be _____? Jesus said 77!
11. Too much stuff to worry about? Try living in _____.
12. _____ comes from a heart devoted to God and to helping others.
14. Sometimes we just have to hold on, but God is with us.

Journey

faith journey (JUHR-nee) *n.* Choosing to grow closer and closer to God; traveling through life as a follower of Jesus Christ; refusing to stay put and stop growing in faith.

Which of the words or SMART goals in this study mean the most to you? Why?

What steps are you ready to take as you continue your journey as a disciple of Jesus Christ?